The Apostolic Tradition Reconstructed:

A Text for Students

PAUL F. BRADSHAW

Emeritus Professor of Liturgy
University of Notre Dame, USA

Contents

The cover illustration, part of the recently discovered Ethiopic manuscript of the *Apostolic Tradition,* is reproduced by permission from Alessandro Bausi et al., 'The Aksumite Collection. . . ', *COMSt Bulletin*, 6/2 (2020), p. 154.

1

Introduction

History of the Scholarship

Within the nineteenth-century search for ancient manuscripts undertaken by western scholars in monasteries and other libraries in Europe and around the Mediterranean, a group of early Christian writings were discovered to which scholars applied the collective term 'Ancient Church Orders', because in various ways and to varying extents they gave instructions about the ethical, institutional, and liturgical life of Christian communities that they appeared to be addressing. All of these church orders claimed in one way or another to be 'apostolic' (see Bradshaw, 2015). One of these finds was first published in full by HenryTattam (1848) from a manuscript in the Bohairic dialect of Coptic dating from as recently as 1804. It had no title or author, and so for want of a better designation it came to be called 'The Egyptian Church Order'. Gradually, much older manuscripts of the same work in other ancient languages were discovered: in the Sahidic dialect of Coptic, Arabic, Ethiopic, and Latin. It became clear that they were all translations of a Greek original, which no longer existed except for a few fragments.

It was also quickly recognized that there was some sort of literary relationship between this particular church order and several others: the *Apostolic Constitutions* and its *Epitome*, the *Canons of Hippolytus*, and the *Testamentum Domini*. What is ironical is that at first nobody proposed that the 'Egyptian Church Order' might be a source from which the rest were derived, but it was unanimously judged to be descended from one or other of those church orders. This verdict was not corrected until the early twentieth century, when it was (mis)identified with what was thought to have been a lost third-century work by a certain Hippolytus of Rome, the *Apostolic Tradition*, first by Eduard von der Goltz (1906) and then in more detailed studies, independently of one another, by Eduard Schwartz (1910) and R. H. Connolly (1916).

Their conclusions rapidly became the established consensus among scholars for most of the twentieth century. Indeed, so sure of the veracity of this theory did many of its supporters become that they claimed to find parallels in theology and vocabulary with other works attributed to Hippolytus and downplayed or simply ignored anything that might raise questions about it (see Bradshaw, 2017). It is true that the occasional voice was heard to challenge the verdict, most notably Rudolf Lorenz (1929) and Hieronymous Engberding (1948), but their views were subjected to heavy criticism. Similarly, E.C. Ratcliffe (1950) asserted that the eucharistic prayer in the church order had been extensively reworked in the fourth century, but his reconstruction of the original was so radical that it failed to win widespread support. In a review published in 1964 he claimed that this reworking had applied to the whole church order: it was 'not Hippolytus's original composition, but an edition of it current in the last quarter of the fourth century' (*Journal of Theological Studies* 15, p. 405); but again his judgement was largely ignored.

The same fate befell the claims made by Antoine Salles (1955), who questioned the Roman character of its baptismal rite; by Jean Michel Hanssens (1959), who argued at great length that the whole work had originated in Alexandria; and by Jean Magne (1965; 1975; 1988), that it was really an anonymous compilation, of which the true title was the *Diataxeis tôn hagiôn apostolôn*, made up of elements from different places and time periods. Unfortunately, as in the case of Ratcliffe, Magne's alternative explanation—that this church order had eventually been fused with a passage from a genuine 'Tradition apostolique sur les charismes' of Hippolytus—was too unconvincing for his theory to win any serious consideration from others.

It was not, therefore, until Marcel Metzger published a series of articles (1988; 1992a; 1992b) developing the idea earlier advanced by Magne and also briefly by Alexandre Faivre (1980, p. 286), that not only was the church order not the *Apostolic Tradition* of Hippolytus, it was not the work of any single author at all but rather a piece of 'living literature', that scholars began to give the claim proper attention. Like Magne, Metzger argued that its lack of unity or logical progression, its frequent incoherences, doublets, and contradictions, all pointed away from the existence of a single editorial hand. Instead, it had all the characteristics of a composite work, a collection of community rules from quite disparate traditions. In the years since then this conclusion has been accepted by an ever increasing number of scholars, although they have continued to retain the name *Apostolic Tradition* for convenience. Alistair Stewart (2001), however, was an interesting exception. He sought to keep as much of the traditional ascription as possible, by building on a theory put forward by Allen Brent (1995) that there was an Hippolytean school of writers at Rome, and arguing that the *Apostolic Tradition* was the work of members of this school over the period from the late second century to the middle of the third, and that this explained the disunity of the text. This time period, however, appears to be too short to account for all the updating that was done to the text; the restriction to Rome fails to account for the variety of liturgical practices within it; and Stewart's division into layers is too subject to the imagined theological views of different members of this supposed school.

Sources

Any edition or translation of the *Apostolic Tradition* is to some extent a work of reconstruction because of the absence of any Greek text, apart from a small number of fragments. The Latin has traditionally been used as the basis for this reconstruction as it is the oldest surviving manuscript, written in the late fifth century and copied from a translation of the Greek thought to be about a century older. It has been judged to provide a very literal translation, but it is incomplete, with significant sections missing. To supplement it, in the past the Sahidic manuscript from the year 1006 seemed next closest to the original, although it deliberately omitted the texts of the eucharistic and ordination prayers and some other chapters. This Coptic dialect had the advantage of using a number of Greek loan words, but the disadvantage of a different grammatical construction from Greek. The Arabic translation was supposedly made in 1295 from an older Coptic text but it may actually have been a little earlier than that. It exists now only in manuscripts dating from the fourteenth to the seventeenth centuries, and it moved even further away from a literal rendering than the Sahidic. The Ethiopic, which survives in manuscripts from the fifteenth to the eighteenth centuries, was made from a better Arabic text than is in the extant Arabic manuscripts, including the preservation of the texts omitted in the Sahidic and Arabic and of other chapters not included in any other versions, but it also features a number of interpolations. The other church orders that used the *Apostolic Tradition* as a source were also able to contribute to discerning a true reading at some points even if at others they diverged widely from it.

The greatest advance in trying to establish the Greek text that ultimately lay behind all the translations, however, came with the publication by Alessandro Bausi (2011) of a different Ethiopic translation of the church order apparently made sometime between the end of the fifth century and the seventh century and preserved in a single manuscript from not later than the fourteenth century. Not only does this furnish another translation besides the Latin that was made at an early date and directly from Greek rather than via an intermediary language but it also corresponds closely to the Latin for much of the church order, indicating that it was made from a similar Greek text. The other translations, on the other hand, apparently all derive from a different textual tradition where the underlying Greek seems already to have undergone some expansion even before the various translators added their own. In order to distinguish it from the other Ethiopic translation, it is often referred to as E1, with its later companion designated as E2.

This means that E1 can now be used as the primary source for the reconstruction of the Greek where the Latin is absent, and even occasionally to correct it when both are present, and because together they represent a quite distinct tradition from the rest, this results in a significantly different, more reliable, and slightly shorter version than has ever been presented before. It needs to be acknowledged, however, although E1 appears largely faithful to the Greek behind it and mostly free from the sort of expansions in the other translations, it does have its textual difficulties in various places as well as some omissions of its own. Until the present work, the only scholars to have made extensive use of E1 have been Reinhard Messner (2016) and Alistair Stewart (2015) in the second edition of his translation and commentary on the *Apostolic Tradition* mentioned earlier, and even he does not base his translation on it in every place where the Latin is missing. Nevertheless, though disagreeing with the context and date in which Stewart sets the original work, I have found his English translation of portions of E1 there and his judgements about the Greek text of the church order useful in the preparation of this volume.

This Reconstruction

Establishing the Greek text is, however, only part of the process of reconstruction. Once one has accepted that the *Apostolic Tradition* as we have it is a composite work, made up of a basic core that has been supplemented and modified by different hands over a period of time from the second to the fourth centuries (and even later in some of the translations), then it becomes necessary to attempt to dissect the existing text to discern what that core might have been, and where in it emendations and expansions might have been made.

Some recent studies of the church order have already suggested specific points in the text where such editorial work seems to have taken place, but this translation is an attempt to make the various chronological layers of the whole document more visually evident to students by the use of three different typefaces. At some points these different layers can be detected with a high degree of confidence, in other passages rather more tentatively.

Often it is vocabulary that provides the guide. In Chapter 3, for example, the prayer uses as a title for Jesus the word 'servant', which had given way to 'Son of God' and other more exalted titles in Christian discourse by the middle of the second century, while elsewhere in that prayer we encounter descriptions of the bishop's office in priestly terms, something that did not come into Christian use until the third century, and of the new bishop 'propitiating' God's countenance, language that belongs more to fourth-century Christianity. Clearly, then, this prayer must have layers of accretion.

In other places it is a significant disagreement between the different translations that is the clue. In Chapter 2, for instance, although all the sources mention the presence of other bishops, and the Latin and E1 obviously both used a Greek text that did so at the same point in the passage, the wide differences in the other translations as to where they introduce this reference is one factor that points to this not having been the earliest form of the Greek text.

This reconstruction cannot claim to be definitive because there are some passages where there is insufficient evidence for a sure judgement to be made. Nevertheless, it is hoped that it will be sufficient to give an idea to readers of just how different the oldest material in this church order appears to have been from the later translations of it, and of the progress from the relative simplicity of the earliest instructions to the more detailed and complex versions designed to meet changed situations and doctrinal beliefs of later ages.

The probable temporal origin of each part of the church order is presented in three broad historical periods. What is thought to be the oldest material, from the second century, is presented in Roman type, words that were subsequently moved or deleted being struck through. This first layer need not have formed a single collection. It could, for example, have consisted of a set of directions about admission to different offices in the church; another document describing how baptisms were to be performed; and some scattered instructions about the eucharistic meal and other aspects of church life, all being subsequently brought together as the first recognizable form of the church order. What are thought to be later (seemingly early- to mid-third-century) additions to this stratum are printed in italics. Within this layer are some parts, particularly the core of prayer texts, that appear as old as the first layer but were only *added* to the church order at this time. Material that is considered to have been inserted even later (belonging mostly to the late-third or early-fourth century) is marked by underlining.

It must be emphasized that each of these categories of material was not the work of just a single editor or redactor, nor were the changes in each band necessarily all made at exactly the same time. The typographical variations simply indicate periods of time in which a number of changes appear to have been made, almost certainly by several different hands. As for the region of the ancient world where this church order originated, all that can be said is that the core of the baptismal material in Chapter 21 with its threefold questions and answers is characteristic of North Africa, evidenced by Tertullian at the beginning of the third century (*De baptismo* 3–4). Rome is another possibility for this, as its liturgical practices tended to resemble those of North Africa, but we lack any confirmation of the form of its baptismal interrogation at this early date. Egypt might also be added, but clear evidence is again unavailable. In any case, whether those baptismal instructions were derived from a pre-existing source (perhaps reflecting a different location) or were newly composed for inclusion in the first draft of the church order is impossible to determine. Much of the rest of the text lacks firm indications of a specific location, but there are elements that point clearly to some of the redaction as having taken place in an Eastern church, as for example, the eucharistic prayer in Chapter 4 (see Smyth, 2011) and the reference to daily pre-baptismal exorcism in Chapter 20.

Words in brackets have been added to help make sense: they are not necessarily a part of the original text that is missing. The Latin once had titles for each chapter, but being written in red ink, they have completely faded, and so the titles from E1 have been used. Different versions also had their individual systems of numbering chapters, but modern editions have created their own. This reconstruction adopts the numbering system generally used nowadays that was devised by Bernard Botte (1963) in his edition and French translation of the text.

Further Reading

Those readers seeking more information about some of the reasoning behind the chronological judgements that have been made here or about other aspects of this church order are encouraged to consult the following in addition to the literature in the Bibliography:

Bradshaw, Paul F., Maxwell E. Johnson, and L. Edward Phillips, 2002, *The Apostolic Tradition: A Commentary*, Hermeneia Commentary Series, Minneapolis: Fortress Press.

Bradshaw, Paul F., 2021, 'The Ordination Prayers in the so-called *Apostolic Tradition*', *Vigiliae Christianae* 75, pp. 119–29.

——— 'Presbyters in the *Apostolic Tradition*', in Bart Koet, Edwina Murphy, Murray Smith (eds), *Presbyters in the Early Church: The First Two Centuries*, WUNT series, Tübingen: Mohr-Siebeck (forthcoming).

Johnson, Maxwell E., 2005, 'The Problem of Creedal Formulae in *Traditio apostolica* 21.12–18', *Ecclesia Orans* 22, pp. 159–75.

Markschies, Christoph, 1999, 'Wer schrieb die sogenannte *Traditio Apostolica*? Neue Beobachtungen und Hypothesen zu einer kaum lösbaren Frage aus der altkirchen Literaturgeschichte', in Wolfram Kinzig, Christoph Markschies, and Markus Vinzent, *Tauffragen und Bekenntnis*, Arbeiten zur Kirchengeschichte 74, Berlin: de Gruyter, pp. 8–43.

Stewart-Sykes, Alistair, 2009, 'The Baptismal Creed in *Traditio Apostolica*: Original or Expanded?', *Questions liturgiques* 90, pp. 199–213.

Stewart, Alistair C., 2020, 'The Ordination Prayers in *Traditio Apostolica*: The Search for a *Grundschrift*', *St Vladimir's Theological Quarterly* 64, pp. 11–24.

Vinzent, Markus, 2020, 'Traditio Apostolica', in Jens Schröter and Christine Jacobi (eds), *The Reception of Jesus in the First Three Centuries* 2, London: Bloomsbury T&T Clark, pp. 539–54..

2

Reconstruction

[1] *¹We have set down those things that are worthy of note about the gifts that God from the beginning according to his own will bestowed on human beings, presenting that image which had been lost. And now led on by love toward all the saints, we have arrived at the summit of the tradition that is proper for all the churches, so that those who have been well taught by our exposition may guard that tradition which has remained up to now, and being aware [of it] may remain firmer, on account of that fault or error which was recently invented through ignorance and those who are ignorant,² since the Holy Spirit bestows perfect grace on those who rightly believe, that they may know how those who preside over the church ought to hand on and preserve all things.*

[2] Concerning the Bishop

³Let him be ordained bishop who has been chosen by all the people, and when he has been named and accepted by all, let *him assemble* the people ~~assemble~~ together with the presbytery *and those bishops who are present*, on the Lord's day. When all give consent, let *them* ~~the presbytery~~ lay

---

¹ Both the Latin and E1 locate this prologue at the beginning, unlike E2, which places it after Chapter 30. The statement was probably composed when the earliest material in the church order was first brought together in a single document.

² It is impossible to determine who these alleged innovators might have been who were challenging the version of traditional practices that the author of this section desired to preserve.

³ The Latin verb *ordinare*, 'ordain', seems to be translating the Greek verb *cheirotoneo*, 'elect by raising the hand', throughout the church order (see *Didache* 15.1). In the oldest version the body of presbyters from the local congregation were to conduct the ordination; later the presence and involvement of neighbouring bishops was added. Cyprian of Carthage in the middle of the third century said that by his day this was done 'in nearly all the provinces' (*Letter* 67.5). In this later version one of the bishops lays his hand on the candidate and says a fixed ordination prayer, which was subsequently expanded as the concept of a bishop changed.

hands on him *and let the presbytery stand by, being still.* And let all keep silence, praying in the heart for the descent of the Spirit; *of whom let one of the bishops present, being asked by all, laying the hand on him who is being ordained bishop, pray, saying thus:*

[3] [4]'*God* and Father of our Lord Jesus Christ, the Father of mercies and the God of all comfort, dwelling on high and looking on that which is lowly, knowing all things before their creation, You, *giving [the] rules of [the]church through the word of your grace, having foreordained from the beginning a righteous race from Abraham, having appointed rulers and priests,* and not leaving your sanctuary without a ministry, having been pleased from the creation of the world to be glorified in those whom you chose; and now *pour forth the power from you of the spirit of leadership, which you gave through your beloved servant Jesus Christ to your holy apostles* who established the church in every place as your sanctuary to the unceasing glory and praise of your name. Knower of the heart, grant *to this your servant whom you have chosen for the episcopate to shepherd your holy flock,* and to serve as high-priest for you blamelessly night and day, unceasingly to propitiate your countenance, *and to offer to you the gifts of your holy church*; and in the high-priestly spirit to have authority to forgive sins according to your command, *to give lots*[5] *according to your bidding,* to loose every bond according to the authority that you gave to the apostles, *and to please you in gentleness and a pure heart, offering you a sweet-smelling savour; through your servant Jesus Christ, through whom*

---

[4] A Greek text of this prayer has been preserved in the fourth-century *Epitome of Apostolic Constitutions* 8, and the translation here is chiefly based on it. The use of 'servant' language about Jesus places its origin no later than the middle of the second century, but the use of New Testament quotations (e.g., 2 Cor. 1.3) and also of 'high-priestly' language about the bishop indicates that there were later additions, as the earliest use of such language is in Tertullian, *On Baptism* 17, written around the beginning of the third century. Note that divisions between Chapters 2 and 3 and between 3 and 4 here are entirely the invention of modern scholars. In all the ancient translations the chapters form a single continuous whole.

[5] Rather than meaning 'assign ecclesiastical duties', as this phrase has often been interpreted, it is perhaps more likely originally to have meant here 'arrange the distribution of food rations' (to the needy). See also a similar phrase in Chapter 30.

[be] glory and power and honour to you, <u>with the Holy Spirit,</u> *now and always and to the ages of ages. Amen.'*

[4] [6]When he has been made bishop, let all offer the mouth of peace, greeting him because he has been made worthy. *And let the deacons bring him the oblation, and let him, laying hands on it with all the presbytery, say, giving thanks: 'The Lord [be] with you.' And let them all say, 'And with your spirit.' 'Up [with your] hearts.' 'We have [them] to the Lord.' 'Let us give thanks to the Lord.' 'It is worthy and just.' And so let him then continue:*
'We render thanks to you, God, through your beloved servant Jesus Christ, whom <u>in the last times</u> *you sent to us as saviour and redeemer and messenger of your will,* <u>who is your inseparable word, through whom you made all things and it was well pleasing to you,</u> *[whom] you sent from heaven into the virgin's womb,* <u>and who conceived in the womb was incarnate and manifested as your Son, born from the Holy Spirit and the virgin;</u> *who fulfilling your will and gaining for you a holy people, stretched out [his] hands when he was suffering, that he might release from suffering those who believed in you;* <u>who when he was being handed over to voluntary suffering, that he might destroy death and break the bonds of the devil, and tread down hell and illuminate the righteous, and fix a limit and manifest the resurrection, taking bread [and] giving thanks to you, he said: "Take, eat, this is my body that will be broken for you."</u>

---

[6] E1 omits this entire chapter, probably because it did not correspond with the eucharistic rite known to the translator. The earliest form of the ordination rite seems to have ended with every-one greeting the new bishop with a kiss. Later a eucharistic prayer was inserted, and in a similar way to the ordination prayer, it was subsequently expanded as Christological doctrine and eucha-ristic theology developed, although it did not come to include the Sanctus, as was happening in several places in the fourth century. What is displayed as its primary text here is what is proposed to have been its oldest (second-century) form, to which some of the later additions indicated might already have been made before it was incorporated into this church order. The presbytery joining with the bishop in laying hands on the bread and wine before the eucharistic prayer is not otherwise attested in ancient Christianity. Both the word 'oblation', to mean the bread and wine, and the opening dialogue of the prayer became common in the third century (see, for example, Cyprian, *On the Lord's Prayer* 31).

Likewise also the cup, saying, "This is my blood that is shed for you. When you do this, you do my remembrance."

Remembering therefore his death and resurrection, *we offer to you the bread and cup, giving thanks to you because you have held us worthy to stand before you and minister to you. And we ask that* you would send your Holy Spirit on the oblation of the holy church, *gathering [us] into one, you will give to all who partake of the holy things[7] [to partake] in the fullness of the Holy Spirit, for the strengthening of faith in truth, that we may praise and glorify you through your servant Jesus Christ, through whom [be] glory and honour to you,* Father and Son with the Holy Spirit, *in your holy church, both now and to the ages of ages. Amen.'*

[5] Concerning the Offering of Oil

[8]*If anyone offers oil, let him render thanks according to the offering of bread and wine—and let him say [it] not word for word but to similar effect— saying:*

'As sanctifying this oil, you give, God, health to those using and receiving [it], whence you have anointed kings, priests, and prophets, so also may it afford strengthening to all tasting [it] and health to all using it.'

[6] Concerning the Cheese and the Olives

Likwise, if anyone should offer cheese and olives, let him say thus:

'Sanctify this milk that has been coagulated, coagulating us also to your love, and let us not depart from your sweetness.'

'[Sanctify] also this fruit of the olive which is a symbol of your richness that you have poured from the tree of life for those who hope in you.'

---

[7] Or, alternatively, it might be translated 'all the holy ones who partake'.

[8] Both here and in Chapter 6, it is not made clear who says the prayer—the one offering or (more likely) the bishop. The prayers in these chapters were probably added at about the same time as the eucharistic prayer. E1 has these two chapters out of place, after Chapter 9, perhaps because the omission of the eucharistic prayer by the translator of E1 had left them isolated between the rite for a bishop and that for a presbyter, or perhaps because they had been accidentally omitted by a scribe and needed to be reinserted afterwards.

15

But in every blessing let there be said, 'To you [be] glory, Father, and Son with the Holy Spirit, in the holy church, both now and always and to the ages of ages.'

[7] Concerning the Presbyter

And when a presbyter is ordained, let the bishop lay the hand on his head, the presbyters also touching [him],[9] *and let him say* according to those things that have been said above, as we have said above about the bishop, *praying and saying:*

'*God* and Father of our Lord Jesus Christ, *look upon this your servant and impart the spirit of grace and of counsel of the presbytery that he may help and guide your people with a pure heart, just as you looked upon your chosen people and commanded Moses that he should choose presbyters whom you filled with your spirit that you gave to your servant.*[10]

And now, Lord, grant the spirit of your grace to be preserved unfailingly in us and make [us] worthy, that believing in you we may minister in simplicity of heart, *praising you through your servant, Christ Jesus, through whom to you [be] glory and power,* Father and Son with the Holy Spirit, *in the holy church, both now and to the ages of ages. Amen.*'

[8] Concerning the Deacon

And when a deacon is appointed, let him be chosen according to those things that have been said above, the bishop alone likewise laying on hands as we have prescribed.

---

[9] This is the sole surviving instance of presbyters laying on hands with the bishop at the ordination of a presbyter in ancient Christianity. It was only through the copying of this instruction from here into the anonymous fifth-century Gallican *Statuta ecclesiae antiqua* that ultimately led to its eventual adoption into Gallican ordination practice and from there into all Western, but not Eastern, rites. Like the ordination prayer for a bishop, this prayer also seems to be an addition to the earliest core of the rite, with the beginning of its second paragraph an even later intrusion, as it does not appear to fit the context. E1 omits the prayer completely.

[10] The biblical reference is to Num. 11.16–17. This is the only extant ancient ordination prayer that defines the presbyterate in this way, later ones understanding presbyters not as counsellors but as subordinates of the bishop.

[11]*In the ordination of a deacon, let the bishop alone lay on hands, because he is not ordained to the priesthood but to the service of the bishop, that he may do those things that are ordered by him. For he is not a participant in the counsel of the clergy, but taking care of and indicating to the bishop what is necessary, not receiving the common spirit of the presbytery, that in which the presbyters are participants, but that which is entrusted to him under the power of the bishop. Wherefore, let the bishop alone make a deacon, but on a presbyter let the presbyters also lay on hands on account of the common and like spirit of the clergy.*

For the presbyter has the power of this alone, that he may receive, but he does not have power to give. For this reason he does not ordain the clergy, but at the ordination of a presbyter he seals while the bishop ordains.

And over a deacon let him say thus:

'God, who created all things and ordered [them] by [your] word, the Father of our Lord Jesus Christ whom you sent to serve your will and manifest to us your desire, *give the* holy *spirit of grace* and caring *and diligence to this your servant whom you have chosen to minister for your church,* and to present[12] in your sanctuary that which is offered to you by your high priest to the glory of your name, *that serving blamelessly in a pure way of life, he may be counted worthy of this high office and may praise you through your ~~servant~~* Son *Jesus Christ* our Lord, *through whom to you [be] glory and power and praise* with the Holy Spirit, *now and always and to the ages of ages. Amen.'*

---

[11] The explanation here of the difference between presbyters and deacons belongs to the third century when priestly language began to be applied to bishops and by extension to presbyters (see, for example, Cyprian, *Letter* 57.3).

[12] The Latin translation breaks off at this point, and does not resume until the middle of Chapter 21. The rest of the prayer here has been reconstructed with difficulty from the less reliable versions in the only other witnesses to this section, the later Ethiopic text (E2) and the *Testamentum Domini*. The prayer is omitted from E1, the Sahidic, and the Arabic. The sacerdotal language probably represents a later expansion of an older prayer.

[9] Concerning Imprisoned Confessors

[13]*The confessors, if they have been in bonds because of the name of Jesus Christ, let them not have the hand laid on them for the diaconate or the presbytery, for he has the honour of the presbytery by his confession. But if he is appointed bishop, let him have the hand laid on him. And if he is a confessor who was not taken before an authority, or punished in bonds, or shut in prison, or condemned by any judgement, but by chance was greatly abused for his Lord or otherwise punished under house arrest, let the hand be laid on him for every office of which he is worthy.*

[14]*And let the bishop give thanks as we said before. It is not absolutely necessary for him to give thanks according to this teaching, but according to his ability. If he is able to give a grand and elevated [prayer], then good; but if something of lesser quality, there is nothing to prevent it, if indeed it is sound and correct.*

[10] Concerning the Widow

[15]When a widow is appointed, she is not to be ordained, but she is chosen by name if it has been a long time since the loss of her husband. If instead she lost her husband a short time ago, let her not be trusted. But if she

---

[13] The order of Chapters 9–14 varies in the different ancient translations. The sequence followed here is that of the Arabic and E2 that has commonly been adopted in modern editions as the most likely original form, but E1 actually has the order 13, 11, 10, 9, and 14, and so challenges that conclusion. The earliest known use of the Geek word *homologētēs*, 'confessor', to describe one who had suffered for the faith occurs in the letter of the martyrs of Lyon in 177 CE (Eusebius, *Ecclesiastical History* 5.2.2–3), but the term *klēros*, 'lot' (see Chapters 3, 30) was not used to mean 'ecclesiastical office, clergy' before the third century. The recognition of confessors as members of the presbytery is not mentioned in any other ancient source.

[14] This paragraph has the appearance of being out of place, as it is unconnected to what has just gone before. It would seem more naturally to belong after the eucharistic prayer and before Chapter 5, but all the versions that survive place it here, so perhaps it was simply an afterthought, especially if the chapter concerning confessors was formerly the conclusion of the section on recognized ministristries.

[15] A formal order of widows is mentioned in 1 Tim. 5.3–16. The Sahidic version expands the argument against widows being ordained: 'But a hand shall not be laid on her because she does not offer up the offering or the liturgy. But the ordination is for the clergy for the sake of the liturgies and the widow is appointed only for the sake of the prayer; and this belongs to everyone.'

is an old woman, her emotions will be under control, because it is the time when passions grow old. Let the widow be appointed by the word, becoming enrolled with the rest, but she does not receive ordination by the hand because she does not teach but is appointed only for prayer, which is allowed to all.

[11] Concerning the Reader
[16]A reader is appointed when the bishop gives him the book. For he is not ordained.

[12] Concerning the Virgin
[17]The hand shall not be laid on a virgin, but her choice alone is what makes her a virgin.

[13] Concerning the Subdeacon
[18] *The hand shall not be laid on a subdeacon, but he shall be named to follow the deacon,* and perform the baptism for the bishop.

[14] Concerning the Gift of Healing
[19]If someone says, 'I received the gift of healing through a revelation', the hand shall not be laid on him, for the work itself will reveal if he has truly received it.

[15] Concerning Those to be Baptized who Come for the First Time
Those to be baptized who come for the first time to hear the Word, before they are admitted into the midst of all the people, let them be brought

---

[16] A Greek text of this chapter has been preserved in the *Epitome of Apostolic Constitutions* 8, and is translated here.

[17] This chapter is not present in E1, and the title and text have been supplied from the Sahidic.

[18] Subdeacons are first mentioned in a letter of Pope Cornelius in 255 (Eusebius, *Ecclesiastical History* 6.43). The addition at the end of the sentence is unique to E1 and may well be a later interpolation.

[19] This chapter is displaced in E1, to a position between Chapters 15 and 16, probably the result of a scribal error of having accidentally skipped over the chapter and needing to insert it later.

first to the teacher. And let them be asked about their activity, for what reason they have come to be admitted. And let those who have brought them be their witnesses as to whether they are able to hear the Word. And let them be questioned about their life: Does he have a wife? Is he a slave? Does his master permit him? If he is the slave of a believer, let him bear witness. If he does not witness in his favour, let him be rejected. If he [the master] is a pagan, teach him to please his master, so there shall be no scandal.

And if there is one who has a wife or a woman who has a husband, let them be instructed to remain with his wife or with her husband. And if there is one who is not married, let him be taught not to fornicate; either let him marry legally or if not, remain as he is. And if there is one who has a demon, let him not hear the word of the teacher until he is purified.

[16] Concerning the Craft and the Profession

[20]*Let it be asked what are the crafts and professions of those who will be admitted. If one is a brothel keeper who is a caretaker of prostitutes, let him abandon this activity or be rejected. If one is a sculptor or a painter, let him be taught not to make idols, and if he refuses, let him be rejected. If he is one who performs in the theatre, let him cease or otherwise be rejected. If he teaches young children, it is good thing for him to cease. If he does not have another profession, let it be conceded.*

Again, one who competes with horses and enters the games, let him abandon this activity or be rejected. A gladiator or an instructor of gladiators, or one who fights with bears, who engages in public combat, let him be rejected. A priest of the idols or a custodian of the idols—that is, one who guards them—let him cease or be rejected.

A soldier who finds himself in a certain authority, let him not kill; and

---

[20] Much of this chapter might have formed an independent list before it was incorporated into this church order. It differs in places from the Sahidic over some categories of people, and over their treatment. E1, for example, expands the reference to a soldier to order him not to sacrifice or wear the wreath. On the other hand, the Sahidic does not allow a repentant prostitute, profligate, or self-castrator to be admitted.

also if he is ordered, let him not offer sacrifice, swear [the military oath], and not put wreaths on the head. One who executes with the sword, or a ruler of a city or one who wears the purple, let him cease or otherwise be rejected. A catechumen or one of the faithful, if he desires to be enlisted [in the army], let him be rejected because he did a wrong to the Lord.

A prostitute or profligate man or one who castrated himself, if he abandons his activity, he can be admitted to hear. Let a sorcerer be rejected, because he does not come under consideration. A magician, one who practises incantations, an astrologer, one who interprets dreams, an enchanter, and one who makes phylacteries, let them cease, or if not, be rejected.

Someone's concubine, if she raised the children that she gave him and is his alone, let her be admitted to hear, and if not, let her be rejected. A man really commits murder if he has a concubine; let him cease and let him marry legally. But if he is unwilling, let him be rejected.

If there is anything that we have overlooked, the fact itself will teach, for we all have the Holy Spirit in us.

[17] On the Time of the Hearers
[21]Let the catechumen be a hearer for three years; but if one is engaged in something and is dedicated with perseverance, it is not judged according to the time, but according to the character.

[18] Concerning the Prayer of the Hearers
Let the catechumens, when they have left the teacher, pray apart from the faithful. And let the women be standing by themselves. Let the faithful not exchange the sign of peace with the catechumens, for they are not yet holy. Let the faithful kiss each other, men with men and women with

---

[21] This chapter is difficult to date. There are no other explicit references to a three-year catechumenate in the Christian literature of the first three centuries, and only a few fourth-century indications of some unsuccessful attempts to extend the catechumenate to a varying numbers of years.

women; they kiss on the mouth.[22]

<u>Let all the women veil themselves with a veil on the head, not with soft linen, for this is not a covering; but the virgins do not veil themselves because their state as a believer is obvious.</u>

[19] Concerning the Imposition of the Hand

Let the teacher, after they have prayed, lay a hand on the catechumens, and after having prayed, let him dismiss them. The one who teaches, even if he is a layperson, let him do so.

[23]*If there is a catechumen who is arrested for the name and perseveres, let him not be in two minds; For if there is a sudden attack and he is killed before he receives his forgiveness, he will have been baptized with his blood and is justified.*

[20] Concerning Those Who Come to be Baptized

[24]When those who are to receive [baptism] have been chosen, after their life has been examined—if as catechumens they lived virtuously, if they honoured the widows, and if they visited the sick, and if they did good works—let those who brought them testify for them, and thus let them hear the Gospel. <u>From the time that they have been chosen, let hands be laid on them in the mornings, exorcising them.</u> *And when the day draws near, let the bishop exorcise each one of them so that he may be sure that*

---

[22] Some early Christian communities segregated the sexes, as here; others did not. E1 is unique among the versions in adding a reference to virgins here.

[23] The status of the execution of catechumens became an issue in the third-century persecution of Christians, and baptism in blood is mentioned by Tertullian (*On Baptism* 16), and more explicitly taught by Cyprian (*Letter* 72.22).

[24] The oldest layer of the baptismal material consisted of a relatively simple set of instructions, with no mention of particular ministers performing specific functions (similar to Justin Martyr's brief description of baptism in his *First Apology* 61). Later, these instructions were expanded in these two chapters (20–21) to indicate the special role of the bishop, who in this chapter now performed an exorcism of the candidates. Exorcism was not a regular part of baptismal rites at first, but reserved for individuals thought to be particularly possessed; and the further reference to a daily exorcism must be a later insertion still, as this was only a feature of Eastern rites from the fourth century onwards (see, for example, Cyril of Jerusalem, *Procatechesis* 9, 13–14).

they have become pure. If any suspicion results, let him be turned away and disgraced because he did not hear faithfully; indeed an alien being cannot reside in him.

Let those who are intended to be baptized be instructed to take a bath on the fifth day of the week. But if there is a woman is menstruating, let her be turned away and let her be baptized on another day. Let those who are to be baptized fast on the day of preparation and the Sabbath.[25] *On the Sabbath let the bishop, after having gathered those who are to be baptized, command them to kneel, and laying his hand on them, let him exorcise [them], saying, 'Let every alien spirit be cast out from them and not return again.' When he has exorcised [them],* <u>let him blow[26] and having signed their foreheads and their ears and nostrils,</u> *let him raise them up.*

[27]In the night let them be read to and be instructed. Let there be no other thing that they bring, those who are to be baptized, except each a loaf for the Eucharist, because it is appropriate for those who participate to offer something at that time.

[21] On Anointing[28]

At the time of cockcrow, let them come to the water. Let the water be flowing or at least running.[29] And let it be so if there is no exigency. If there is concern about an exigency, do it with any water.

---

[25] That is, on Friday and Saturday. *Didache* 7 mandates a pre-baptismal fast of one or two days.

[26] That is, he blows on the candidates' faces to drive away the alien spirits, a pre-baptismal practice first attested in a letter of a certain 'John the Deacon' written from Rome sometime around the year 500, as also is the sealing of the forehead and orifices.

[27] This reference to a vigil lasting until cockcrow does not necessarily imply that the baptism was being conducted at Easter.

[28] A surprising title for the baptismal rite, which in the Sahidic version is called 'Concerning the Tradition of Holy Baptism'.

[29] 'Living' water was always preferred at first by early Christians, as it was a place where the Holy Spirit was thought to dwell (see *Didache* 7). It was only when domestic pools or water tanks became the more usual location for baptism that prayer for the Spirit to come upon the water became necessary, as in the Sahidic version; see also Terullian, *On Baptism* 4.

So let them take off their clothes. Give precedence to the small children and baptize them; let those who are able reply, or alternatively let their parents or another one from their family reply; afterwards, the grown men; and finally the women, loosening the hair and laying aside their jewellery. Let no one have anything with them, while they go down into the water.

[30]*When they are to receive the oil of exorcism, let the bishop give thanks over a vessel and let him exorcise another.*

[31]Let a deacon take the exorcised oil and stand near the presbyter; similarly the other, the oil of thanksgiving. Let him stand on the right, and the presbyter who exorcises stand on the left. Let him take them one by one and ask if he believes. Let him [the candidate] say, 'I renounce you, Satan, all your works, all your service, and all your contamination.' And once he has declared his profession, let him be anointed with the oil of exorcism, pronouncing [the words] for the purification from every alien spirit. *Thus, let him deliver him to the bishop* or the presbyter, *to the one who baptizes him,* [the candidate] *standing naked in the water.* Let the deacon also go down with him into the water.

And when the one who is being baptized goes down into the water, let the one who baptizes him say, 'Do you believe in one God Almighty?' Let the one who is being baptized say, 'I believe.' [32]Having [his] hand laid on his head, let him baptize [him] once. And afterwards let him say, 'Do you believe in Christ Jesus, the Son of God, who was born of the Holy Spirit from[33] the Virgin Mary and crucified under Pontius Pilate, and died and was buried and rose on the third day alive from the dead, and

---

[30] The simple directions, which would originally have gone straight on to the contents of the questions and answers, are here interrupted by directions about the actions of the bishop and exoristic anointing that were later inserted into the rite.

[31] The fusion of directions as to how a bishop is to preside at a baptism with other directions as to what a presbyter is to do when presiding instead has resulted in lack of clarity as to what actions were previously performed by the bishop in this section.

[32] The Latin returns at this point. There has been some debate whether the answer to the second question was integral to the church order, or a later expansion: see the Appendix, pp. 42–46.

[33] E1 reads 'and of' rather than 'from'. It is more likely to be the original rather than the Latin.

ascended into heaven and sits on the right hand of the Father, and will come to judge the living and the dead?' And when he has said, 'I believe', let him be baptized again. And again let him say, 'Do you believe in the Holy Spirit and the holy church and the resurrection of the flesh?' Then let the one who is being baptized say, 'I believe', and let him be baptized a third time.

Concerning the Anointing with Balsam[34]

And afterward, when he has come up, let him be anointed by the presbyter with that oil which was sanctified, saying: 'I anoint you with holy oil in the name of Jesus Christ.'

And so individually drying themselves, let them now dress and afterward enter into the church.[35] *And let the bishop, laying [his] hand on them, invoke, saying, 'Lord God, who have made them worthy to receive the forgiveness of sins through the washing of regeneration of the Holy Spirit, send on them your grace, that they may serve you according to your will, for to you is glory,* Father and Son with the Holy Spirit, *in the holy church, both now and to the ages of ages. Amen.'*[36]

Afterward, pouring the sanctified oil from [his] hand and placing [it] on the head, let him say, 'I anoint you with holy oil in God the Father Almighty and Christ Jesus and the Holy Spirit.' And signing [him] on the

---

[34] Only E1 inserts a new heading here, using the word 'balsam' rather than 'sanctified oil', as in the body of the text. Post-baptismal anointing was a feature of some third-and fourth-century rites (see, for example, Tertullian, *On Baptism* 7). The fusion of what a bishop was to do at baptism with what a presbyter was to do when presiding instead has resulted in the appearance of a double post-baptismal anointing.

[35] 'Church' here almost certainly means the assembly of the people and not a church building.

[36] There has been much debate over the original form of this prayer. The wording adopted here follows the Latin translation. The other versions, including E1, render it instead along the lines of 'Lord God, who have made them worthy to receive the forgiveness of sins through the washing of regeneration, make them worthy to be filled with your Holy Spirit and send on them your grace....' Although this latter form is preferred as the original by a number of scholars, it seems more likely that later redactors would have converted it to a prayer for the gift of the Holy Spirit when that was beginning to be associated with a post-baptismal anointing in Eastern churches in the fourth century, rather than the Latin translator altering it in the opposite direction: see, for example, (Cyril of Jerusalem?,) *Mystagogical Catecheses* 3.1, 3.

forehead, let him offer [him] a kiss and let him say, 'The Lord [be] with you.'
And let the one who has been signed say, 'And with your spirit.' Let him do
this to each one.

And afterward let them pray together with all the people, not praying
with the faithful until they have carried out all these things. And when
they have prayed, let them offer the peace with the mouth.

And then let the oblation be presented by the deacons to the bishop
and let him give thanks over the bread <u>for the representation of the body</u>
<u>of Christ,</u> *and over the cup of mixed wine* <u>for the representation of the</u>
<u>blood that was shed for those who believe in him; and milk and honey[37]</u>
<u>mixed together for the fulfilment of the promise that was made to the</u>
<u>fathers, which said, 'I will give a land flowing [with] milk and honey', and</u>
<u>which Christ gave as his flesh, through which, like little children, those</u>
<u>who believe are nourished, the gentleness of his word making sweet the</u>
<u>bitterness of the heart; and water for an offering as a sign of washing,</u>
<u>that the inner person also, which is the soul, may receive the same as the</u>
<u>body. And let the bishop give an explanation about all these things to</u>
<u>those who receive.</u>

And breaking the bread [and] distributing individual pieces, let him
say, 'Heavenly bread in Christ Jesus.' And let the one who receives respond,
'Amen.' <u>And if the presbyters are not sufficient, let the deacons also hold</u>
<u>the cups, and let them stand in good order: first the one who holds the</u>
<u>water, second the one who [holds] the milk, third the one who [holds] the</u>
<u>wine. And let those who receive taste of each, three times, the one who</u>
<u>gives saying, 'In God the Father Almighty.' And let the one who receives</u>

---

[37] Milk and honey were given to the newly baptized after they received their first communion in
North Africa from the beginning of the third century onwards (see Tertullian, *On the Chaplet* 3),
but the particular arrangement here (bread, water, milk mixed with honey, wine) is highly idio-
syncratic and fused with what seems to be part of a baptismal catechesis in the rest of the chapter.

say, 'Amen.' 'And in the Lord Jesus Christ.' And let him say, 'Amen.' 'And in the Holy Spirit and the holy church.' And let him say, 'Amen.' So let it be done with each one.

And when these things have been done, let each one hasten to do good works pleasing to God, and to live uprightly, devoted to the church, doing the things that he has learned, advancing in the service of God.

[38]It is therefore fitting to be given this in brief on the washing and on the offering, because they have already been taught. But concerning the resurrection of the flesh and concerning everything according to the Scriptures, as is convenient, let the bishop reveal and explain at the time when they are to be baptized, in contrast to what is given to catechumens. This is the white stone of which John said that on it is a new name that no one knows except the one who is baptized.[39]

[22] [40]And on the Sabbath *and on the first [day of] the week let the bishop with his own hand, if it is possible, distribute to all the people, as the deacons break [the bread].* And let the presbyters break the baked bread. And if the deacon offers to the presbyter, let him spread out his garment, and let him [the presbyter] take. But he [the deacon?] distributes to the people with his hand. And on the other days let them receive as the bishop has ordered.

---

[38] The Latin breaks off again here.

[39] Rev. 2.17.

[40] This somewhat confusing chapter exists only in the two Ethiopic versions, but there are echoes of it in two other church orders that use *Apostolic Tradition* as a source, the *Canons of Hippolytus* and the *Testamentum Domini*. Although E1 simply refers to the Sabbath alone and E2 to Sunday as well, both the Ethiopic versions also locate the ordination of a bishop on a Saturday. Thus, it seems reasonable to suppose that E1 'corrected' an original Sunday to Sabbath, and E2 added it. Eucharistic celebrations on Saturdays were a fourth-century development in Eastern churches. There appears to have been some disagreement as to whether deacons or presbyters were to perform the fraction, and the addition of the word 'baked' does nothing to clarify the situation. Some scholars change 'garment' to 'paten', which is the reading adopted in the *Testamentum Domini*.

[23] On Fasting

[41]Let the widows <u>and the virgins </u>fast often, and let them pray for the church. Let the presbyters fast when they wish, and likewise lay people. A bishop is not able to fast except when all the people [fast]. For it happens when someone wishes to offer, he is not able to refuse, <u>but having broken, he always tastes.</u>

[24] On What is Given to the Sick

[42]Let the deacon <u>in an emergency</u> give the sign to the sick promptly <u>if there is no presbyter,</u> and when he has given, as soon as possible let him take from what has been distributed and consume it straightaway.

[43]Concerning the One who Takes to Serve

Let him give the blessing diligently. If someone takes a gift which is to be given to a widow or to a sick person or one who is occupied with work for the church, let him bring it on that same day. And if he does not, let him bring it on the following day, after adding something of his own, because the bread of the poor remained with him.

---

[41] Another chapter where a Greek text survives, strangely in just one manuscript of the *Epitome* of *Apostolic Constitutions* 8, and is translated here. The last clause appears to be a version of the beginning of Chapter 26, which is what follows immediately in all the translations except the Ethiopic ones. There is no explicit mention here of the regular weekly fast days for everyone (Wednesdays and Fridays) which are known to have existed in many Christian communities from early times (see *Didache* 8).

[42] This chapter and the next two exist only in Ethiopic, but allusions to these chapters in the *Canons of Hippolytus* and the *Testamentum Domini* imply that a version of them was once a genuine part of this church order. Although the text of this chapter in E2 is unintelligible, the earlier Ethiopic version (E1) is much clearer. In Chapter 34, it is the deacon, not the presbyter, who is primarily responsible for the care of the sick, which is why the reconstruction suggests that preference for the presbyter is a later addition. The 'sign' or 'seal' usually refers to anointing or to baptism, but that seems very unlikely here, though if it did, the priority given to the presbyter would make more sense. The next sentence, however, suggests it was something to eat.

[43] E1 introduces a new chapter heading here, although the first sentence seems to belong to the previous paragraph. The word 'blessing' refers to blessed bread (see the end of Chapter 28), which clarifies what was given to the sick in the previous paragraph.

[25] On the Bringing in of the Light

[44]At the [Lord's] Supper, when the bishop is present, after evening has come, let the deacon bring in the lamp, and after standing among the faithful who are there, let him[45] give thanks. *Let him first offer a greeting thus, saying: 'The Lord [be] with you.' And let the people say: 'And with your spirit.' 'Let us give thanks to the Lord.' 'It is right and just.' But let him not say, 'Up with your hearts', because it is said at the oblation.. And let him pray: 'We give you thanks, O God, through your Son Jesus Christ our Lord, through whom you have enlightened us, revealing to us the light that does not perish. Having, therefore, finished the length of the day and arrived at the beginning of the night, having been filled with the light of the day that you created for our satisfaction, and now, as we do not lack the evening light by your grace, we praise you and glorify you through your Son Jesus Christ our Lord, through whom [is] glory, might, and honour with the Holy Spirit, now and always and to the ages of ages. Amen.*

[46]And let the faithful who are present at the Supper take from the bishop's hand a small piece of bread before they break their own bread. <u>For this is a blessing and not the Eucharist like the body of our Lord.</u>

---

[44] Like the previous two chapters, this one only exists in the Ethiopic versions. The version in E2 continues after the end of the first paragraph with further material that shows every indication of being a much later interpolation by the translator. Tertullian's account of a Christian supper (*Apologeticum* 39) places the bringing in of the light after the supper and not before it, which is what seems to be intended here.

[45] Probably the bishop rather than the deacon.

[46] This paragraph and the following chapters give instructions for what appears to have been the early eucharistic meal prior to the Eucharist being moved to the morning and the eucharistic prayer in Chapter 4 being added. It seems that a later redactor has tried to make it clear that this meal was not to be understood as a Eucharist, although elsewhere in the church order 'blessing' does mean the eucharistic bread: see Chapter 24 and the end of 28.

[26] On the Supper

[47]Before they all drink, once they have washed [their hands], it is fitting that those who are present taste of the cup over which thanks have been given, [48]and so feast. But to the catechumens let exorcised bread be given and let each one help themselves to a cup.

[27] On the Catechumens: Let Them not be Together [with the Faithful]

Let a catechumen at the Lord's Supper not sit together [with the faithful]. But through the whole meal, let the one who eats be mindful of the one who invited him, because for that reason he requested that he should enter under his roof.[49]

[28] Concerning that You are Orderly and Moderate

[50]*When eating and drinking, do it with moderation and not to the point of drunkenness and ridicule, or that the one who invited you blame himself because of your disorderliness, but that he may be pleased to have been worthy that saints may enter in to him, for 'You', he said, 'are the salt of the earth.'[51] And if a portion is offered in common to all (which is called*

---

[47] Although E1 places the chapter division here, the other versions, perhaps more rationally, place it before the previous paragraph, but their actual title 'Concerning the Time of Eating' does not seem appropriate. E1 is alone in referring to the washing of hands before the meal, although it is treated by Tertullian as a standard practice after the meal and before the bringing in of the light (*Apologeticum* 39).

[48] The Latin also returns here, oddly in the second person plural, but otherwise confirms E1.

[49] Cf. Matt. 8.8; Luke 7.6. The context here implies that the Lord's Supper was held in the home of a member of the local church who supplied the contents of the meal.

[50] The first part of this chapter changes from third person to second person plural, suggesting it is an addition from another source. For similar advice about good manners when eating and drinking, see Clement of Alexandria, *The Instructor* 2.2. E1 has been used here to help clarify the Latin.

[51] Matt. 5.13.

in Greek *apophoreton*[52]), take it. *But if it is so that all may eat, eat with moderation, so that some may remain and the one who invited you may send [it] to whomever he wishes, as from the leftovers of the saints, and may rejoice at your coming.*

And let those who are invited to eat, do so in silence, not contending with words, except when the bishop allows, and if he asks anything, answer shall be given him. And when the bishop says a word, let everyone remain modestly silent, until he asks again.

[53]Even if without the bishop the faithful are at supper with a presbyter or deacon present, let them similarly eat appropriately. And let everyone hasten to receive the blessing from the hand, whether from a presbyter or from a deacon. Similarly, a catechumen shall receive it exorcised. If the laity are together, let them act with moderation, for a lay person cannot make the blessing.

[29] Concerning that They are to Receive with Thanksgiving
[54]Let everyone eat in the name of the Lord. For this is pleasing to God, that we should be envied among the peoples, all alike and sober.

---

[52] This clause was obviously added by a translator. The Greek word means a gift to take away.

[53] It seems from the words about the catechumens receiving the blessing 'exorcised' that 'blessing' here originally did not mean simply 'words of blessing', as later translators understoood it, but had to be the eucharistic bread. This passage must have predated the third century, as by then a deacon would not have given a blessing, still less presided at the Eucharist. It coheres with the instruction by Ignatius of Antioch in the second century that the Eucharist was to be 'administered either by the bishop or by one to whom he has entrusted it' (*Letter to the Smyrnaeans* 8), and is similar to the statement by Tertullian that the right to confer baptism rested with the bishop, and then with presbyters and deacons with the bishop's authorization (*On Baptism* 17).

[54] If the first part of Chapter 28 were a later addition, this short chapter would have been the sole reference to conduct at the supper in the earliest text. The reference to thanksgiving in the title is absent from the content of the chapter in both the Latin and E1.

[30] Concerning the Supper of the Widows

[55]If someone wishes to feed the widows *already mature in age, after they have eaten* let him dismiss them before evening. But if this is not possible because of the lot he has been assigned, giving them food and wine, let him send them away and let them partake of it at their own homes, as it pleases them.

[31] Concerning the Fruit that it is Proper to Offer

[56]Let each one hasten bring to the bishop the fruits of the first harvest; and let the one who offers bless [them] and name the one who brought [them], saying: 'We give thanks to you, God, and we bring to you the first of the fruits that you have given us to eat, [you] nourishing them by your word, ordering the earth to bear all fruits for the enjoyment and nourishment of people and for all animals. For all these we praise you, God, and in all things with which you have benefitted us, adorning for us the whole creation with varied fruits, through your servant Jesus Christ *our Lord*, through whom to you [be] glory to the ages of ages. Amen.'

[32] The Blessing of Fruits

[57]*Fruits indeed are blesssed, that is, grape, fig, pomegranate, olive, pear, apple, mulberry, peach, cherry, almond, plum; not pumpkin, not melon, not cucumber, not onion, not garlic, or any of the other vegetables. But sometimes flowers are brought.* Therefore let the rose and the lily be offered, but not others.

---

[55] The Latin adds *already mature in age* and E1 *after they have eaten.*The other translations have references to both. For the distribution to widows, see Chapter 24; and for the use of the word 'lot', Chapter 3.

[56] The prayer itself does not explicitly name the one who brought the fruits, as the preceding words instruct. Does this mean that it could be secondary addition, like the other prayers in this church order? This chapter deals with a subject prominent in primitive Christianity (see *Didache* 13). The titles of this and the following chapter appear to have somehow become reversed.

[57] This strangely limited list of what may be offered has the appearance of a secondary insertion. The further limitation of flowers to the rose and the lily may be because Christians viewed them as Messianic symbols (see, for example, Cyprian, *Letter* 8.5). Just before these two are named, the Latin had a new heading, now illegible.

And in all things that are eaten, let them give thanks to the holy God, eating to his glory.

[33] On not Eating Anything before the Proper Time at the Pascha
[58]At the Pascha let no one eat before the oblation has been made. For whoever does so, for him the fast does not count. But if anyone is pregnant or sick and is not able to fast for two days, let them fast on the Sabbath because of [their] necessity, confining [themselves] to bread and water. *If anyone finding himself at sea or in some necessity did not know the day, when he learned of this, let him observe the fast after Pentecost. For the type has passed, because it ceased in the second month, and he ought to fast when he has learned the truth.*

[34] That it is Proper for the Deacons to Attend on the Bishop
[59]Let each deacon *with the subdeacons* attend on the bishop. Let him also be told who are sick, so that, if it is pleasing to the bishop, he may visit them. *For a sick person is greatly consoled when the high priest remembers him.*

[35] [Concerning the Hour when it is Proper to Pray]
[60]Let the faithful, as soon as they have woken and risen, before they touch their work, pray to God and so hasten to their work. And if there is any instruction in the word, let him give preference to this so that he hurries and hears the Word of God for the comfort of his soul. Let him hasten to the church, where the Spirit flourishes.

---

[58] Fasting on Friday and Saturday in preparation for Pascha (Easter) was one of several alternative practices already established before the end of the second century, but the Christian season of Pentecost is unknown before the beginning of the third century The final sentence directs that any who were unaware of the correct date for Pascha should not keep it in the second month, which had been prescribed for those being unable to keep the Passover on the due date in Num. 9.9–12.

[59] The office of subdeacon and the use of the term 'priest' or 'high priest' to denote the bishop only emerge from the third century onwards: see above, notes 4, 11, 18.

[60] This chapter is present in the Latin, though missing from E1, the title being supplied here from the Sahidic. The word 'church' is not used in reference to a building before the third century, but it may simply mean the congregation here.

[36] Concerning that it is Proper to Receive the Eucharist Before Anything

[61]*Let every faithful [person] try to receive the Eucharist before he tastes anything. For if he receives in faith, even if someone may give him something deadly after this, it will not overpower him.*

[37] Concerning that the Eucharist should be Watched over Diligently

[62]*Let everyone take care that an unbeliever does not taste of the Eucharist, nor a mouse or any other animal, nor that any of it falls and is lost. For the body of Christ is to be eaten by the faithful and not to be despised.*

[38] Concerning the Cup, that it should not be Spilled

[63]*For having blessed the name of God, you received it as the antitype of the blood of Christ. Therefore refrain from pouring out [any], as if you despised [it], so that an alien spirit may not lick it up. You will be guilty of blood, as one who scorned the price with which he has been bought.*

[SHORTER ENDING]
[Title?]

Always try to sign your forehead reverently. For this sign of the Passion is displayed against the devil, if anyone is to do [it] with faith, not to please human beings but through knowledge presenting [it] as a breastplate. When the adversary sees the power of the Spirit from the

---

[61] A Greek version of this chapter has survived in an eighth-century collection of patristic quotations and is translated here. Although some of the ancient translators understood it to concern the reception of communion at the Eucharist, this and the following chapter really seem to be about receiving communion daily at home from consecrated bread brought from the Sunday celebration, a common practice in the third century (see, for example, Tertullian, *To his Wife* 2.5).

[62] As noted above, this concerns the proper preservation of the consecrated bread at home for daily communion there.

[63] Because of the change from the usual third person to the second person, this chapter apparently comes from a different—though equally ancient—source, and seems to refer to the less common custom of taking consecrated wine home to be consumed daily there.

heart clearly displayed in the likeness of baptism, he will flee trembling, with you not striking him but breathing [on him].[64] This is what Moses [did] typologically with the lamb that was sacrificed at the Passover: he sprinkled the blood on the threshold and anointing the two doorposts,[65] signified that faith in the perfect lamb that is now in us. Signing the forehead and eyes with the hand, let us escape from the one who is trying to destroy us. And so, when these things are heard with thankfulness and true orthodox faith, they provide edification for the church and eternal life for believers. I instruct that these things be kept by those who are wise. For to all who hear the apos. . . . [66]

[LONGER ENDING]

[**39**] [67]*And let the deacons with the presbyters gather in the early morning where the bishop has commanded, and let the deacons not miss being present always, unless they are prevented by an illness. Once they have gathered, let them tell it to the church, and so, after praying, let each one do what is right.*

---

[64] For this reference to baptismal practice, see above, note 26.

[65] Ex. 12.7, 22–3.

[66] This material, which is extant only in the Latin in an incomplete form, seems to belong to the same genre, if not the same source, as the catechesis at the end of Chapter 21. Scholars are generally agreed that the Latin translator was familiar with a shorter version of the church order that ended at the missing conclusion of this passage, although our reconstruction has suggested that the earliest material had been even shorter. The translator then combined his shorter text with a longer version that he also possessed to produce the full church order as we have it.

[67] This chapter, missing from the Latin, runs on directly without heading from Chapter 38 in E1 and the Sahidic. It is a different version of Chapter 34, where presbyters are substituted for subdeacons. The Arabic and E2 understand the word 'tell' (which was used in Chapter 34 of the deacons informing the bishop concerning those who were sick) to be 'teach' and so interpret the occasion, not just as a meeting of deacons with the bishop, but as an early morning assembly of the people for instruction and prayer.

[40] Concerning the Cemeteries

[68]*Those who are buried in the cemeteries, let them not overcharge them, for this work is done for the poor; only the wage for the gravedigger and the price of the tiles. And let those who take care of the place and live there be supported by the bishop, so that it shall not be a burden for those who come.*

[41] Concerning the Prayer

[69]*And let every faithful man and woman, at dawn when they have arisen from sleep, before doing anything, wash their hands and pray to the Lord, and so let them go to their work. But if it happens that there is instruction in the word of God, let each one always prefer to go there; let each one acknowledge to himself that he is hearing the universal word of the Lord; for having been seen in the church, you will be able to evade the evil of the day. Let the one who fears God therefore consider this a loss when he is not present at the proclamation of the word of instruction, or when the only one who can read arrived late, or the teacher comes.[70] Do not leave the church while the instruction is being held, because then it is given to the speaker to say what will be profitable for all. While the Spirit gives [you] things you do not hope for, having heard, you will benefit and your faith will become firm through what has been said, and in your home say what you have heard. Because of this, let each one hasten to the church, where the Spirit flourishes. If there is a day when instruction is not held, let him also read in his home something from holy Scripture as far as is possible.*

---

[68] A chapter with no parallel in the shorter version, and missing from the Latin. In E1, on which this reconstruction is based, it is placed at the end, after Chapter 43, perhaps because a scribe had accidentally omitted it at its proper place and needed to add it subsequently.

[69] A greatly expanded version of Chapter 35. The composite character of the first paragraph can be seen from the mixture of the third person plural, third person singular, and second person singular. Possibly as a result of this fusion, the meaning of some expressions is opaque.

[70] There seems no convincing explanation for the last part of this sentence.

⁷¹*At the time of the third hour, while you pray, if you are in your house, praise the Lord; if in another place, pray in your heart to God, having paid attention to the particular time, because at that hour we welcome Christ's return. Because of this also the Law commands that they offer the type of the lamb and of the bread in the image of the perfect lamb, Christ the shepherd, who is the bread of heaven.*⁷²

*So likewise at the sixth hour, for once Christ had been nailed [to the cross], the day divided and there was darkness*⁷³ *Because of this, let prayer be continued, like the voice of the one who prayed and that of the prophets, while the creation became dark for unbelievers.*

At the ninth [hour] let the prayer be prolonged with praise because we are united in praising while the soul of the righteous praise ⁷⁴*God, who does not lie, who was mindful of his saints and sent his Word to illuminate them. Therefore at that hour Christ, pierced in his side, poured forth water and blood,*⁷⁵ *and illuminating the rest of the time of the day, he brought [it] to evening. Then, beginning to sleep [and] making the beginning of another day, he completed an image of the resurrection.* Pray also before your body rests on the bed.⁷⁶

---

⁷¹ Instructions for a pattern of daily prayer begin here. Three times each day are prescribed, at the third, sixth, and ninth hours, an arrangement known in other early sources (for example, Clement of Alexandria, *Miscellanies* 7.7.40), here being linked chiefly to moments in Christ's crucifixion. Although E1 is not always easy to comprehend in this chapter, it is significantly briefer than the Sahidic here, showing how much the text was expanded as it progressed to the latter translation.

⁷² See Ex. 12; 25.30; John 1.29; 10.11; 6.32–3.

⁷³ See Mark 15.33.

⁷⁴ The Latin version resumes at this point and forms the basis of the reconstruction in the rest of the chapter.

⁷⁵ John 19.34.

⁷⁶ Prayer at bedtime (as distinct from the evening) is first attested in some fourth- and fifth-century monastic rules.

[77]*And rising about midnight, wash your hands with water and pray. And if your wife is also present, pray both together; but if she is not yet a believer, withdrawing into another room, pray and return again to your bed. And do not be lazy about praying.* <u>The one who is bound in marriage is not defiled. For those who have washed do not have necessity to wash again, because they are clean. Through consignation with moist breath and catching your spittle in your hand, your body is sanctified down to your feet. For when it is offered with a believing heart, just as from the font, the gift of the Spirit and the sprinkling of washing sanctifies the one who believes.</u>[78] *Therefore it is necessary to pray at this hour. For the elders who handed [it] on to us taught us so, because at this hour all creation is still for a moment, so that they may praise the Lord: stars and trees and waters stop for an instant, and all the host of angels [that] ministers to him praises God at this hour together with the souls of the righteous. Therefore those who believe ought to take care to pray at this hour. Also bearing witness to this, the Lord says thus, 'Behold, a shout was made about midnight of those saying, "Behold the bridegroom comes: rise to meet him."' And he goes on, saying, 'Therefore watch; for you do not know at what hour he comes.'*[79]

[80]<u>*And rising about cockcrow, likewise. For at that hour, when the cock crowed, the sons of Israel denied Christ, whom we know by faith, looking toward this day in the hope of eternal light at the resurrection of the dead.*</u>

And acting thus, all you faithful ones, and making a remembrance of them and in turn teaching and encouraging the catechumens, you will not be able to be tempted or to perish, when you always have Christ in remembrance.

---

[77] Prayer in the middle of the night normally accompanied the pattern of threefold prayer during the day, it being a common custom in the ancient world to break the time of sleep into two parts. Tertullian (*To his Wife* 2.5) expresses concern about what a pagan husband might think his Christian wife was doing when she rose in the night to pray.

[78] This section interrupts the directions about prayer at midnight and so seems to be a later interpolation.

[79] Matt. 25.6, 13.

[80] Prayer at cockcrow was practised by some fourth-century monastic communities instead of prayer at midnight (see, for example, Egeria, *Itinerarium* 24.1).

[42] [81]Always take care to sign your forehead reverently. For this sign of the Passion is clear and approved against the devil, if you do it with faith, not so that you may be seen by people but through knowledge presenting [it] like a breastplate. For when the adversary sees the power that is from the heart of a person clearly displayed in the likeness of the washing, he will flee trembling, not by spitting but by breathing. This is what Moses earlier showed with the lamb of the Passover that was sacrificed, who sprinkled the blood on the lintels and smeared the doorposts, so he made known the faith that is now in us, which is in the perfect lamb. And signing the forehead and eyes with the hand, let us escape from the one who is trying to destroy us.

[43] And so, if these things are received with thankfulness and true faith, they provide edification for the church and eternal life for believers. I instruct that these things be kept by all the wise. For to all who listen to the apostolic tradition,[82] the heresies will not be able draw any righteous one into error. For heresies have increased in this way because of you lacking the apostolic tradition, the leaders who love the doctrine and who abandon themselves to various passions of their own desire, not those things that are proper. (If we have abbreviated anything, our brothers, may God reveal [it] to those who are worthy, as he steers the holy church into the tranquil harbour.)

---

[81] This and the following chapter constitute another version of the shorter ending above after Chapter 38. The translation from the Latin has been modified by reference to E1.
[82] The Latin breaks off again here. What follows has been conjectured largely on the basis of E1, which unfortunately makes little sense as it stands. The final sentence is not present in E1 and has been drawn from the other versions.

3

Appendix:

The Expansion of the Baptismal Creed

As observed in Chapter 21 with regard to the threefold questions and answers at the time of baptism, there has been some debate as to whether the longer version there was a later interpolation or a genuine part of the church order. The discovery of the Ethiopic translation (E1) has settled that particular matter, because it includes the same wording as the Latin, which therefore confirms that the Greek text being used by both translators contained the full form. However, a further question still remains. Was this full form part of the earliest version of the church order, or does it belong to a later expansion of the second question from what had previously been in a short form similar to those to the first and third questions? In other words, would the question originally have simply read: 'Do you believe in Christ Jesus?'

There are several reasons to suppose that all three answers had originally been in a short form. First, the oldest form of prayers throughout the church order describe Jesus as God's servant and not as God's Son. Thus, the Christology of the longer second answer is too advanced for the period to which we are assigning the earliest layer of this document. Second, there is evidence of the use of such short responses in other early baptismal sources, and in particular in Ambrose of Milan (c. 340–397):

You were asked, 'Do you believe in God the Father Almighty?' You said, 'I believe', and you were immersed, that is, you were buried. Again you were asked, 'Do you believe in our Lord Jesus Christ, and in his Cross?' You said, 'I believe', and were immersed, therefore, you were also buried with Christ; for the one who is buried with Christ, rises again with Christ. A third time you were asked, 'Do you believe also in the Holy Spirit?' You said, 'I believe', and were immersed a third time (Ambrose, *De sacramentis* 2.7.20; see also *De mysteriis* 28).

Indeed, the baptismal questions and answers in the Roman Rite down to the eighth-century Gelasian Sacramentary reveal a less amplified form than in the *Apostolic Tradition*:

> Do you believe in God the Father Almighty?
> R. I believe.
> And do you believe in Jesus Christ his only Son our Lord, who was born and suffered?
> R. I believe.
> And do you believe in the Holy Spirit; the holy Church; the remission of sins; the resurrection of the flesh?
> R. I believe.

What seems to have happened, therefore, is that a redactor of the *Apostolic Tradition* expanded the original short answers to correspond more closely to an early version of the Apostles Creed known as the Old Roman Symbol, which was emerging in both Greek and Latin during the fourth century, but cast it artificially in interrogatory form to fit the context.

> I believe in God the Father almighty;
> and in Christ Jesus his only Son, our Lord,
> who was born of the Holy Spirit and the Virgin Mary,
> who under Pontius Pilate was crucified and buried,
> on the third day rose again from the dead,
> ascended to heaven,

sits at the right hand of the Father,
From where he will come to judge the living and the dead;
and in the Holy Spirit,
the holy Church,
the remission of sins,
the resurrection of the flesh
(the life everlasting).[1]

The translators of the church order into other ancient languages went further in incorporating credal material that was familiar to them into these baptismal statements. The Sahidic preceded the first immersion with a short credal declaration of its own before turning the second and third baptismal questions of its source into a longer creed.

'I believe in the only true God, the Father, the Almighty, and his only begotten Son, Jesus Christ our Lord and Saviour, with his Holy Spirit, the giver of life to everything, three in one substance, one divinity, one Lordship, one kingdom, one faith, one baptism, in the holy catholic apostolic church, which lives forever. Amen.'

And the one who receives it, let him say to all this, 'I believe thus.' And the one who gives will put his hand on to the head of the one who receives and dip him three times, confessing these things each time. And afterwards, let him say:

'[Do] you believe in our Lord Jesus Christ, the only Son of God the Father, that he became man wondrously for us in an incomprehensible unity in his Holy Spirit from Mary, the holy virgin, without human seed; and he was crucified for us under Pontius Pilate; he died willingly for our salvation; he rose on the third day; he released those who were bound; he went up to heaven; he sat at the right hand of his good Father in the heights; and he comes to judge the living and the dead by his appearance with his kingdom.

> And [do] you believe in the Holy Spirit, the good and the giver of life, who purifies the universe in the holy church . . .'[2]
> Again let him say, 'I believe.'

The Arabic and the later Ethiopic (E2) are very similar the Sahidic. The two church orders that use the *Apostolic Tradition* as a source here, the *Canons of Hippolytus* and the *Testamentum Domini,* both also expand the preliminaries. The *Canons* requires candidates to face west for the renunciation of evil or, as it is termed in Eastern rites, the *apotaxis;* and then, after being anointed with the oil of exorcism, to face east for the *syntaxis,* a feature of Eastern baptismal rites used there rather than a credal interrogation: 'I believe and submit myself to you and to all your service, O Father, Son, and Holy Spirit.' Then follows a redundant set of credal questions derived and adapted from the *Apostolic Tradition,* fused with the baptismal formula that had emerged at an early date in Syria before being adopted in Egypt.

> 'Do you believe in God the Father Almighty?' He who is baptized replies, 'I believe.' Then he immerses him in the water once, his hand on his head. He questions him a second time, saying, 'Do you believe in Jesus Christ, Son of God, whom the Virgin Mary bore by the Holy Spirit, who came for the salvation of the human race, who was crucified in the time of Pontius Pilate, who died and was raised from the dead the third day, ascended into heaven, is seated at the right hand of the Father and will come to judge the living and the dead?' He replies, 'I believe.' Then he immerses him in the water a second time. He questions him a third time, saying, 'Do you believe in the Holy Spirit, the Paraclete flowing from the Father and the Son?' When he replies, 'I believe', he immerses him a third time in the water.

And he says each time, 'I baptize you in the name of the Father, of the Son, and of the Holy Spirit, equal Trinity.'

The *Testamentum Domini* similarly has each candidate turn west for a more detailed *apotaxis*: 'I renounce you, Satan, and all your service, and your theatres, and your pleasures, and all your works.' Then after the exorcism, they face east for a similar expanded *syntaxis*: 'I submit to you, Father and Son and Holy Spirit, before whom all nature trembles and is moved. Grant me to do all your wishes without blame.' This is followed by a similar version of the threefold questions and answers to that in the *Canons*, but without the added baptismal formula.

Endnotes

1. Cited from J.N.D. Kelly, 1950, *Early Christian Creeds,* London/New York: Longmans, p. 100. The final line occurs only in the Greek version.

2. A leaf has been torn out of the manuscript at this point, and so the end of this is missing. The conclusion is supplied from the later Bohairic translation. All quotations from *Apostolic Tradition* 21 and its derivatives in this appendix are taken from P.F. Bradshaw, M.E. Johnson, and L.E. Phillips, *The Apostolic Tradition: A Commentary*, Hermeneia Commentary Series, Minneapolis: Fortress Press, pp. 114–19.

Bibliography

Bausi, Alessandro, 2009, 'The "so-called *Traditio Apostolica*": Preliminary Observations on the new Ethiopic Evidence', in Heike Grieser and Andreas Merkt (eds), *Volksglaube in antiken Christentum*, Darmstadt: Wissenschaftliche Buchgesellschaft, pp. 291–321., 2011, 'La nuova versione Etiopica della *Traditio Apostolica*: edizione e traduzione preliminare', in Paola Buzi and Alberto Camplani (eds), *Christianity in Egypt: Literary Production and Intellectual Trends*, Studia Ephemeridis Augustinianum 125, Rome, pp. 19–69.

Botte, Bernard, 1963, *La tradition apostolique de saint Hippolyte: Essai de reconstitution*, Liturgiewissenschaftliche Quellen und Forschungen 39, Münster: Aschendorff, ⁵1989.

Bradshaw, Paul F., 2015, *Ancient Church Orders*, Alcuin/GROW Joint Liturgical Study 80, Norwich: SCM-Canterbury Press., 2015, 'Conclusions Shaping Evidence: An Examination of the Scholarship Surrounding the Supposed Apostolic Tradition of Hippolytus', in Paul van Geest, Marcel Poorthuis, and Els Rose (eds), *Sanctifying Texts, Transforming Rituals: Encounters in Liturgical Studies*, Leiden: Brill, pp. 13–30.

Brent, Allen, 1995, *Hippolytus and the Roman Church in the Third Century: Communities in Tension before the Emergence of a Monarch-Bishop*, Supplements to Vigiliae Christianae 31, Leiden: Brill.

Connolly, R.H., 1916, *The So-called Egyptian Church Order and Derived Documents*, Cambridge: Cambridge University Press; reprinted 1967, Nendeln, Liechtenstein: Kraus.

Golz, Eduard von der, 1906, 'Unbekannte Fragmente altchristlicher Gemeindeordnungen', *Sitzungsberichte der königlich preussischen Akademie Wissenschaften* 56, pp. 141–57.

Engberding, Hieronymous, 1948, 'Das angebliche Dokument römische Liturgie aus dem Beginn des dritten Jahrhunderts', in *Miscellanea liturgica in honorem L. Cuniberti Mohlberg* I, Rome: Edizioni liturgica, pp. 47–71.

Faivre, Alexandre, 1980, 'La documentation canonico-liturgique de l'Eglise ancienne', *Revue des sciences religieuses* 54, pp. 204–19, 237–97.

Hanssens, Jean Michel, 1959, *La Liturgie d'Hippolyte: Ses documents, son titulaire, ses origines et son charactère*, volume 1, Orientalia Christiana Analecta 155, Rome, ²1965; volume 2, 1970.

Lorenz, Rudolf, 1929, *De egyptische Kerkordening en Hippolytus van Rome*, Haarlem: J. Enschedé.

Magne, Jean, 1965, 'La prétendue Tradition apostolique de Hippolyte de Rome s'appelait-elle *Ai diataxeis tôn hagiôn apostolôn*, "Les statuts des saints Apôtres"?', *Ostkirchliche Studien* 14, pp. 35–67., 1975, *Tradition apostolique sur les charismes et Diataxeis des saints Apôtres*, Paris., 1988, 'En finir avec la "Tradition" d'Hippolyte!', *Bulletin de literature ecclésiastique* 89, pp. 5–22.

Messner, Reinhard, 2016, 'Die angebliche *Traditio Apostolica*: eine neue Textpräsentation', *Archiv für Liturgiewissenschaft* 58/59, pp. 1–58.

Metzger, Marcel, 1988, 'Nouvelles perspectives pour la prétendue Tradition apostolique', *Ecclesia Orans* 5, pp. 241–59., 1992a, 'Enquêtes autour de la prétendue Tradition apostolique', *Ecclesia Orans* 9, pp. 7–36., 1992b, 'A propos des règlements écclesiastiques et de la prétendue Tradition apostolique', *Revue des sciences religieuses* 66, pp. 249–61.

Ratcliffe, E.C., 1950, 'The Sanctus and the Pattern of the Early Anaphora', *Journal of Ecclesiastical History* 1, pp. 29–36, 125–34., 1966, 'Apostolic Tradition: Questions concerning the Appointment of the Bishop', *Studia Patristica* 8, pp. 266–70.

Salles, Antoine, 1955, 'La "Tradition apostolique" est-elle un témoin de la liturgie romaine?', *Revue de l'histoire des religions* 148, pp. 181–213.

Schwartz, Eduard, 1910, *Über die pseudoapostolischen Kirchenordnungen*, Strasbourg: Trübner.

Smyth, Matthieu, 2011, 'The Anaphora of the So-called "Apostolic Tradition" and the Roman Eucharistic Prayer', in Maxwell E. Johnson (ed.). *Issues in Eucharistic Praying in East and West*, Collegeville: Liturgical Press, pp. 71–97.

Stewart (-Sykes), Alistair, 2001, *Hippolytus: On the Apostolic Tradition*, New York: St Vladimir's Seminary Press, ²2015.

Tattam, Henry, 1848, *The Apostolical Constitutions or the Canons of the Apostles in Coptic with an English Translation*, London: Oriental Translation Fund.

Alcuin/GROW Joint Liturgical Studies

The following is a list of the titles published in this series by Hymns A & M; all (except double-size ones) are between 48 and 64 pages. Nos 1-58 were published by Grove Books Ltd, Ridley Hall Road, Cambridge CB3 9HU, and a complete list of those can be found on www.jointliturgicalstudies.hymnsam.co.uk, where you can also order past editions.

1   Roger Beckwith, *Daily and Weekly Worship – Jewish to Christian* (1987)
2   Paul Bradshaw (ed), *The Canons of Hippolytus* (1987)
3   Colin Buchanan (ed), *Modern Anglican Ordination Rites* (1987)
4   James Empereur, *Models of Liturgical Theology* (1987)
5   Thomas Talley (ed), *A Kingdom of Priests: Liturgical Formation of the People of God* (1988)
6   Colin Buchanan (ed), *The Bishop in Liturgy: An Anglican Symposium* (1988)
7   Phillip Tovey, *Inculturation: The Eucharist in Africa* (1988)
8   Paul Bradshaw (ed), *Essays in Early Eastern Initiation* (1988)
9   John Baldovin, *The Liturgy of the Church in Jerusalem* (1989)
10   Donald Withey, *Adult Initiation* (1989)
11   John Fenwick, *'The Missing Oblation': The Contents of the Early Antiochene Anaphora* (1989)
12   Paul Rorem, *Calvin and Bullinger on the Lord's Supper* (1989)
13-14   (double-volume) W. Jardine Grisbrooke, *The Liturgical Portions of the Apostolic Constitutions: A Text for Students* (1990)
15   David Holeton (ed), *Liturgical Inculturation in the Anglican Communion* (1990)
16   Douglas Davies, *Cremation Today and Tomorrow* (1990)
17   Adrian Burdon, *The Preaching Service – the Glory of Methodism* (1991)
18   David Power, *Irenaeus of Lyon on Baptism and Eucharist* (1991)
19   Grant Sperry-White, *The Testamentum Domini: A Text for Students* (1991)
20   Gordon Jeanes, *The Origins of the Roman Rite* (1992)
21   Bosco Peters, *The Eucharist in New Zealand* (1992)
22-23   (double-volume) Ed Foley, *Music in the Early Church* (1992)
24   Paul James, *Eucharistic Presidency* (1993)
25   Ric Barrett-Lennard, *The Sacramentary of Sarapion of Thmuis: A Text for Students* (1993)
26   Phillip Tovey, *Communion Outside the Eucharist* (1993)
27   David Holeton (ed), *Revising the Eucharist: Groundwork for the Anglican Communion* (1994)
28   David Gitari (ed) *The Kanamai Statement 'African Culture and Anglican Liturgy' with Introduction, Papers read at Kanamai and a First Response* (1994)
29-30   (double-volume) Anita Stauffer, *On Baptismal Fonts: Ancient and Modern* (1994)
31   Fritz West, *The Comparative Liturgy of Anton Baumstark* (1995)
32   Alan Kreider, *Worship and Evangelism in Pre-Christendom* (1995)
33   Maxwell Johnson, *Liturgy in Early Christian Egypt* (1995)
34   Timothy Turner, *Welcoming the Baptized* (1996)
35   Diana Karay Tripp, *Daily Prayer in the Reformed Tradition: An Initial Survey* (1996)
36   Edward Phillips, *The Ritual Kiss in Early Christian Worship* (1996)
37   Peter Doll, *'After the Primitive Christians': The Eighteenth Century Anglican Eucharist in its Architectural Setting* (1997)
38   Paul Bradshaw, *Coronations Past, Present and Future* (1997)
39   David Holeton (ed), *Anglican Orders and Ordinations* (1997)
40   Phillip Tovey, *The Liturgy of St James as Currently Used* (1998)
41   Mark Dalby, *Anglican Missals* (1998)
42   Gordon Jeanes, *The Origins of the Roman Rite Vol. 2* (1998)
43   Juliette Day, *Baptism in Early Byzantine Palestine* (1999)
44   Cesare Alzati (tr. George Guiver), *Ambrosianum Mysterium: The Church of Milan and its Liturgical Tradition Vol. 1* (1999)
45   Bryan Spinks, *Mar Nestorius and Mar Theodore the Interpreter: The Forgotten Eucharistic Prayers of East Syria* (1999)
46   James Smith, *The Eucharistic Theology of the Later NonJurors* (2000)
47-48   (double-volume) Cesare Alzati (tr. George Guiver), *Ambrosianum Mysterium: The Church of Milan and its*

Liturgical Tradition Vol. II (2000)
49   Baby Varghese, *The Syriac Version of the Liturgy of St James: A Brief History for Students* (2001)
50   Graham Kings and Geoff Morgan, *Offerings from Kenya to Anglicanism: Liturgical Texts and Contents, including 'A Kenyan Service of Holy Communion'* (2001)
51   Alistair Stewart-Sykes and Judith Newman, *Early Jewish Liturgy: A Source Book for use by Students of Early Christian Liturgy* (2001)
52   Martin Connell, *Church and Worship in Fifth-Century Rome: The Letter of Innocent I to Decentius of Gubbio: Latin Text and Translation* (2002)
53   Alex Hughes, *Public Worship and Communion by Extension* (2002)
54   Colin Buchanan, *The Savoy Conference Revisited* (2003)
55   John Gibaut, *Sequential or Direct Ordination? A Return to the Sources* (2003)
56   Mark Dalby, *Infant Communion: From the New Testament to the Reformation* (2003)
57   David Hebblethwaite, *Liturgical Revision in the Church of England 1984-2004: The Working of the Liturgical Commission* (2004)
58   Trevor Lloyd and Phillip Tovey, *Celebrating Forgiveness: An Original Text drafted by Michael Vasey* (2004)
59   Juliette Day, *Proclus on Baptism in Constantinople* (2005)
60   Donald Gray, *Prayer Book Crisis in the Church of England Part 1: Ritual, Royal Commission and Reply to the Royal Letters of Business* (2005)
61   Donald Gray, *Prayer Book Crisis in the Church of England Part 2: The cul-de-sac of the 'Deposited Book'...until other order be taken* (2006)
62   Ian Tarrant (ed), *Anglican Swahili Liturgies* (2006)
63   David Holeton and Colin Buchanan, *A History of the International Anglican Liturgical Consultations 1983-2007* (2007)
64   Colin Buchanan, *Justin Martyr on Baptism and Eucharist* (2007)
65   Christopher Irvine (ed), *Anglican Liturgical Identity* (2008)
66   Anthony Gelston, *The Psalms in Christian Worship: Patristic Precedent and Anglican Practice* (2008)
67   Mark Dalby, *Infant Communion from the Reformation to the Present Day* (2009)
68   Colin Buchanan (ed), *The Hampton Court Conference and the 1604 Book of Common Prayer* (2009)
69   Trevor Lloyd, James Steven and Phillip Tovey, *Social Science Methods in Contemporary Liturgical Research: An Introduction* (2010)
70   Alistair Stewart, *Two Early Egyptian Liturgical Papyri: The Deir Balyzeh Papyrus and the Barcelona Papyrus* (2010)
71   Kenneth Stevenson (ed), *Anglican Marriage Rites: A Symposium* (2011)
72   Andrew Atherstone, *Charles Simeon on the Excellence of the Liturgy* (2011)
73   Alan Griffiths, *Ordo Romanus Primus: Latin Text and Translation* (2012)
74   Trevor Lloyd (ed) *Rites Surrounding Death: The Palermo Statement with Commentary* (2012)
75   Mark Dalby, *Admission to Communion: The Approaches of the Late Medievals and the Reformers* (2013)
76   Dominic Keech, *Gaudius of Brescia on Baptism and the Eucharist* (2013)
77   Thomas O'Loughlin (ed), *Liturgical Language and Translation: The Issues Arising from the Revised Translation of the Roman Missal* (2014)
78   Paul Bradshaw and Juliette Day, *Further Essays on Early Eastern Initiation* (2014)
79   Phillip Tovey, *Eighteenth Century Anglican Confirmation: Renewing the Covenant of Grace* (2015)
80   Paul Bradshaw, *Ancient Church Orders* (2015)
81   Tim Stratford (ed), *The Richard III Reinterment Liturgies* (2016)
82   David Wallingford (ed. Gordon Jeanes), *The Decalogue in the Reformation Liturgies* (2016)
83   Neil O'Donoghue, *Liturgical Orientation: The Position of the President of the Eucharist* (2017)
84   James Steven, *Ambrose of Milan on Baptism: A Study of De Sacramentis and De Mysteriis* (2017)
85   Stephen R. Shaver, *Eucharistic Sacrifice as a Contested Category: A Cognitive Linguistics Approach* (2018)
86   Thomas McLean, *The Spirit in Liturgy and Doctrine: A liturgical-systematic dialogue in the fourth century church in Egypt and Cappadocia* (2018)
87/88 Colin Buchanan and Trevor Lloyd, *The Church of England Eucharist 1958-2012* (2019)
89   William Smith, *The Use of Hereford: A Medieval Diocesan Rite Reconsidered* (2020)
90   Phillip Tovey, *Inculturating Liturgy in Sri Lanka* (2020)

Subscriptions

Annual subscription: £15 UK   £22 Worldwide

Joint Liturgical Studies is published twice a year, in May and October. Subscribe today to receive the next two issues direct to your home or office.

Call us: +44 (0)1603 785 910
Visit our website: jointliturgicalstudies.hymnsam.co.uk

Or complete this form and send it to:
Joint Liturgical Studies, Hymns Ancient & Modern, 13a Hellesdon Park Road, Norwich NR6 5DR

☐ I enclose a cheque for .... payable to Hymns Ancient & Modern Ltd.

Title................. First name..

Surname..

Address..

....

....

Postcode................................   Tel no..

Email..

How may we contact you?
We would like to keep you up-to-date with news and related offers from the Hymns Ancient & Modern Group. Please tick if you are happy for us to contact you: ☐ by mail ☐ by email ☐ by telephone